Though what we commonly consider sacred in religious terms is referenced in this moving and love-filled collection, that tradition is eclipsed by a higher, wider, and more ethereal reach. The poems here provide a record of the poet's always sudden and brief yet bright encounters with that unknown mystical realm—the texture of water as it falls against the shore, the sound of a snapped tree branch, the recollection of a childhood walk to school and the influence of weather on the meaning of such a walk. All common enough, one may say, but the richness of observed detail in these crisp poems is coupled with formal skill, wisely measured ambiguity, some wry off-hand humor, and plenty of wit. For my reading, that adds up to a fine, uncommonly absorbing book, one that tilts the somber toward affection and the grave toward delight.

—Maurice Manning

www.blacklawrence.com

Executive Editor: Diane Goettel
Cover Design: Zoe Norvell
Cover Art: "White Pine: Crystal River—mid-stream" by Ladislav Hanka
Book Design: Amy Freels

Published 2024 by Black Lawrence Press.
Printed in the United States.

To Leave for
Our Own Country

John Linstrom

for Monique,
who changes everything

Contents

Mouth o' River

Michigan

Liturgy of Next Door

I remember when everything mystical
was connected. The dark repeating *tuh-thump*

of car tires on the highway at night,
the way they changed their rhythm nearing home,

related to the raucous thumps of warped old pews
as grown-ups stood before the gospel, or

the random pops and clicks I'd hear, sitting
weekdays in the empty church next door, between

notes, practicing for lessons on the boxy upright
Everett piano. When the power went out

in the parsonage, the tall clay kerosene lamp,
which I had always assumed was decoration, lit

the dining room, the wide cloth wick so slowly
consumed, and that fire entubed in glass

might have been the same eternal flame
that lived in red glass hanging left

of the altar next door. My dad explained
that when the candle got too low, the new

was lit with the old one's flame, so that's how
it could be eternal. I asked, what if when they're changing

there's a breeze? Someone left the window
cracked? That, he said, and smiled, also

happens. It's just a candle, John.
Sometimes, sitting on a rotty log, the wind

would come from over the church parking lot
down the chilly mud of the ravine, and toss

my hair, and might remind me of the candle
in the red glass tube, or the fluty music

of the Shadowfax cassette we played at night, or the weight
and lightness of the history when I first walked around

the columned, busted, marbled university library
in another town. I didn't name the chill

I'd feel at times, my momma rocking
in the living room chair, my eyes closed, sick,

or poppa typing in his office next door, up the stairs,
stacks of papers leaning silent every step;

I only knew it had to do with darkness
and repeating beats, with something coming home.

Mouth o' River

Ravines stream like oil between dune hips
and each creek trickles exultant—muds ooze,
leaf shade shivers, frogs stretch feeling—all in
to where the sandy land spreads its legs

and the Black River, thick with seaweed sway,
smiling, slides its winding way across the bare
tree ankles and, in sudden shock of sun,
in heavy welcome humid summer air

it sends itself to ecstasy of horizon, into
bands of green vivacious lake life open
to never-ending blue on blue, coming finally
from river's mouth to water wilderness.

A pond skimmer feathers where the bodies join
to shudder their translucent skin. Bark canoes
swish across the sand bar, heading in for home.
Leap of herring, kingfisher dive. For centuries

this dance would never know a dredge,
but they would force one: newcomers
stamping up the Monroe Trail who cut
trees down to the knees to raise their cabin

on the bluff, to sweep a wide survey, a thirsty gaze
up the river's full, lazing length, to name the place.
What love made they that night? Did they cry out
to far Chicago? Back then, did wolves howl too?

Storm's Breath

Sand grits between our teeth, water
strands our hair into cords
that stab eyes

and I see her run
through flocks of seagulls
panting mad sweater-wet

to thud into fresh-toweled me—and I pull
her down too hard, sand blown compact,
cloud-cold. Distant booms: she snickers, we lie,

and every time the waves hiss back
a million tiny worms
peek out of holes to breathe

and then slip back. Their world,
water. And breath. And water
again. Her sweater's rise and fall,

her shiver-laugh. Lake Michigan,
a professor once said, rises
for twenty years, and falls the same,

and no one understands
these bidecadal breaths, sweeping
homes from shorelines every forty years

when the water's belly is biggest.
Then exhale. I wipe away a spear
of her hair but just smear sand.

When summer ends, I can't know
what state we'll be in, whether
we'll remember these whitecaps

and worm fizz, the pale shocks
that stab mid-lake, coming nearer,
the sweatshirt clouds, the smell of rain.

Starburn

But if a man would be alone, let him look at the stars.
The rays that come from those heavenly worlds,
will separate between him and what he touches.
—R. W. Emerson

So unlike you and me, once trapped,
two supermassive stars
in binary attraction
will slide through easy space,
meet in the middle, violent
and silent as candle flames, and wed:

a new creature, collision rite,
pulsing, flashing whole.

We're not trapped. We're spread,
spread-eagle on pine needles
under black-green whispers
and eyelids thin as flames.

I cannot conceive
in the dark, the space
between our mouths, which is vast
or negligible, as between our ages,

vast or negligible. The average star
is forty-one fifty light-years
from the next, and our sparky Sun
should live to thirteen billion.

Billion. You're not so old,
nor I, comparably, so young.
I imagine the debris of my chattering
teeth should have reached you by now.

Feet become miles,
hands become roots,
and under each smile
we're bare-boned and soot.

Soot, pastors have said,
thick-thumbed and sober, into my head:

> *Soot of a palm frond,*
> *soot of a young star;*
> *of soot you were first formed*
> *and sooty you still are,*

on my head, scratched and spread
by a roving grubby fingernail.
Now that spot's a piney itch
and I just think we're more than carbon

when the wind hits,
less than solar but more than us,
and we quiet as the thinnest needles
fill our minds with a million slender sighs.

What's in a dream but our least-tested wishes,
and what's in a wish but a let-down? The stars
were holes in my memory
of a moment that never could happen.

But this morning, let me recall
that feeling your breath
when you leaned over me,
stale and lovely, I could fall

up through your darkest matter,
your teacher's smile,
the needles of your irises
the whispered net that held me
from so many years of colored light.

Church of the Epiphany

I passed a stained-glass-windowed church each day
walking to Central Elementary School,

midway between the vinyl-sided white
where Maddie, spaniel sentinel, would bark

at all but us, front paws to windowsill,
and the bricked-up edifice of School,

half its corridors forbidden, fire-marshalled,
home of mold, asbestos, mystery.

We'd walk those halls in later years, rehearsal
vagabonds from *Bye Bye Birdie*, piratic,

and sift through boxed-up rotary phones, lift
transmitter, lean into receiver, take

whichever one had weathered best the words
of students to their parents, old ones now

to dead. But by the stained-glass-windowed church
that squatted at the corner, a fourth-grade boy

with sandy hair and too-big glasses turned
each day, bouncing palm-sized rubber balls,

and paused sometimes at dusk to see the colors
streaming wrong-ways into the garden—

a monkish statue leaned, his hand a sign
that read of age, of silence, stone, and night.

Dear Shadow

It is long since we talked, since we walked
the Hudson like we used to. Long since

the rabbits in the bushes watched us darkly
as we hopped together, you dropping,

like a reflection, down the sidewalk glare.
I walked another river today, through

a latticework cast by trees, a cool breeze.
I didn't notice you. Water frothed

on rocks I could not see. Limbs creaked
in the wind, and I said something

to my companion about the fangs of the earth.
I stepped, snapped a branch, and smiled

in some way darkly familiar. I wonder now
if you were there, smiling along,

a snap that breaks out in the woods and is gone.

What Was Precious

I remember ladybugs and sow bugs precious
as father's green coffee canteen, as mother's

running shoes. I remember warty toads
and worms with skin like ours, rainy days

when they'd take to the walks, their bodies splayed
so earnest and unheeding over concrete

I could gather them by the tens, scolding them,
water running in my eyes and filling up their homes.

Summer nights were cicada whir, froggy peeps,
traffic and the smell of grass. Once, we're told, night held

wolves, howls of shaggy ghosts, and pigeons,
orange breasts mottling a mile-long, feathered cloud.

I imagine the pigeons descend, tornadic, a roar
of grease-beaked benediction, apocalyptic vision

that I only once saw approximated by bats
funneling down the autumnal evening air

to christen, unwelcomed, mother's white legs,
her skirt swung, our hands raised in joy.

Another Small Town Drowning

South Beach Parking Lot

Rage captivates; sorrows bore.
As winter storms the banded, woolly sky,
seagulls huddle gravely on the shore.

On radios drone the newsmen, rich and poor,
to share a summons, raise a battle cry.
Rage captivates. Your sorrows bore.

Papers fill the glovebox, strew the floor.
Diesel engines idle, time to bide.
Seagulls huddle gravely on the shore,

and drivers drag their cigarettes or snore.
The dreamers know what radio amplifies,
that rage will captivate, that sorrows bore.

The child who dared the pier, the wave that tore
echo through the dune grass as a sigh
where seagulls huddle, gray against the shore.

The town returns each night in waves for more,
dashboards lighting faces too far-tried,
knowing rage will captivate whom sorrows bore.
The seagulls huddle gray against the shore.

Retting

After the gathering,
the pluck from dirt,
rip of root from root—

before the breaking down,
the *scutch-scutch* of knife
against fibers hung

and before the heckle comes
to comb proverbial wheat
from chaff—

we must rot
from the inside:
    free the best fibers,
    make ready the linen.

Graduates

Indiana, Iowa

Motherly Influence

My mac & cheese has plasticized
overnight; the fluorescent light's
too bright as I set the noisy coffee pot.

I sip night's blackness by the window
after showering, my hair become familiar-clean
and soft as sunflower petals in the yard.

I have her hair. These walls feel heavy,
and the morning half-light hits them
so they flame in auburn, maybe beige—they take

the sepia burn of ancient photos and I'm filled
with dazzles of reflections, undervalued
and overstated, glints of costume jewelry.

We drink coffee though it tires us,
we love our partners and in loving
we forget our work. Mother who loves me,

who shares my hair and made my lunches,
I'm alone and I don't know
what to do with mornings.

Pumpkin on the Porch

1

Sitting on the porch, I watched a red leaf waft in
and light on the orange pumpkin as if to accuse me

of my lateness. Soon the neighborhood would be full
of pumpkins carved so long their faces would fall

in through their noses. *Quite*, said the leaf,
late. I pondered this. One needs a knife.

The best detail is brought by the dull ones
with rounded edges, safe. Real pumpkin knives.

I had no pumpkin knives. But then again,
meat knives work about as well, and satisfy.

2

Then again, to carve a pumpkin without company
is strange. My neighbors down the road

might have mentioned they'd be carving this weekend.
Yet a pumpkin is truly large. What if I walked

the whole way to their other porch to see
two well-carved smiling Jacks stare back, or worse,

no one home? And me,
with this pumpkin weighing on my chest.

3

I think I'd like to smash this gourd and leave
the wet remains on the stoop, like kids

did it. I'd like to feel the soft quash
and the seeds like atoms popping, let my knuckles ring

for the fun of it. But then again I'm not sure
what kids use to smash pumpkins: a sledge, a bat, or what.

I'd have to change my clothes, and the laundry's in the basement.
Now the neighbor's watching from across the road,

and anyway, with the red leaf it looks somewhat nice,
picturesque in the slanting light, and tired.

Leaving the Party

My mind this morning stung with carpet burn,
red but matching not in depth or sheen

the crabapple hanging outside my window,
compact and dark, beetle-shelled.

After a moist night the chill day
half-encased it in thick glints, white frost,

the sunny side remaining rawest red,
so morning brought a bleeding moon.

We danced like satellites, I think, last night,
spinning, the Christmas lights in our glasses,

our bottles. We turned, our toes twisted
in socks in carpet, caught

glimpse of hair, sweatshirt sleeve,
glint of eye or painted nail. The record

skipping, popcorn bursting, fingertips
brushing fingertips, it made us woozy –

warm – sated – Merry
Christmas – see the holly, smell the wine in me,
we're both the mistletoe and needle-tree.

I wonder if the stars could say, clouded
as they were last night when I left

and there was no moon but your face
rising and your body waxing,

your thanks-for-coming to an event forever
ending, why we were so full.

Was the importance in a glance,
distant, half-lidded,

in a compact thank-you,
dark and beautiful, or in a million midair

snowflakes shining
under streetlights, like headlamps

under cloud cover, like something
other than us?

From your stoop this morning,
sipping bitter darkness in the sun,

you might remember
the silence of taillights,
lovely crawl of bodies,

intoxicating hum now stilled and hung
to collect the morning frost.

Losing Track of the Conversation

1

I'm not sure what you said then, who prompted it,
but your mouth was agape, enough that I started from my seat

and didn't fall back. I lifted, tumbled forward toward your mouth
and into it, my shoes nicking the fronts of your teeth

which stood like baleen monuments before the dark portal
of who-knows-what. Your mind swilled through you.

Taste buds cast dark shadows and went on budding
into roofs of houses, into treetops I brushed with one hand

as I passed, causing ripples. I, myself, held—
a hard bit of callousness—but this planet unfurling

shuddered cell by cell. Mailbox, chimney, shrub. I thought to gather them,
but the earth curved away beneath my line of flight.

2

Outer space, as much as you contained,
was a place to hang and fly. I felt clean,

shooting, a shard among grander things
that seemed a crowd in the distance, a fuzziness

like lint, or a drawer of beads I was falling toward
but never reaching. I might have been

a loose collection of such beads strung
when I was struck by the meteor you sent.

3

Snowy dirtball. I flew apart,
cells to atoms and atoms to else,

and entered the background haze. How many years
I flew apart, deteriorating at near the speed of light,

who knows? I flew straight along the felty fabric
of space-time, but space-time curved around again

until I saw myself closing in on me,
all the linty stars backing my wild particles

like teeth around some open spout,
and out! I came to sit again, a little spent,

all my pieces gathered across from you at the table,
not quite sure what I had said.

Lingerer

Dream

The desert conjures
before you, melts
feet to sweat
with reflected rays—

you think the oxygen tube
followed for miles,
glimmering spittle-like,
should liquify. Climb the rise.

In caldera: metal cot
nestled by boulders,
far from spring or fountain,
warm skin folded loose over bone

> *(maybe she's your grandma, maybe
> your girlfriend—the cancer's
> in the bones)*

—last evidence of neglect.
You ask, "How's the oxygen?"
You have no right. She smiles.

Clouds, cool breeze: your distance
slacks, leaves scatter
your mind, you see
her skin sheet away—the tube

coils and lifts her bodiless head
to sway in swirling newspaper wind—
screaming obituaries—her smile
waxy, her eyebrows desperate, as if to say

> *Oh no, I never felt better, and thank you*
> *for walking all this way. It feels*
> *so good, so good honey, to fall*
> *from that racket-body. Can you believe*
> *the steady company of dumb rocks, feel*
> *the love in dying, taste the sugar*
> *of thin blood-iron? You know there was*
> *a symphony in my lungs, a cannon*
> *of my eyes, bagatelle of beating*
> *heart in breast – yes the oxygen!*
> *But tell me, can you? Won't you wake*
> *and fear my ghost? I'm an undressed*
> *snake of medicine! I wonder where*
> *my script is headed – say the Wasting:*
> *We will slink in shame and trembling,*
> *dark rooms are our bane! Ode, ode,*
> *honey why won't you sing? The morphine's*
> *clouding up my music – shift your weight*
> *and breathe with me – the cancer's*
> *in the bones, the bones!*

Wake

The outside dark had gathered in the curve
of that benighted ceiling. I was lost

in someone else's living room. The yawning
arches overhead had room for you

right where I did not want you—echoes hung
like shaking cobwebs—not your voice at all.

I could have curled my spine inside my palm
I had become so small, while casketed

somewhere you were growing smaller too.
The sleeping bag too warm, the hanging night

refusing to give voice, the silver slash
of streetlight or of you—a bagatelle

remembered or imagined—somewhere embalmed—
an ode I ought to write for you, an ode

but what of cobwebs and this darker stuff
can come but fear of rousing oxygen

into the spectral form of that which you
have never been, the mocking acid caw

of blackbirds, constellations rotated
into a blown-out image, pattern gone.

You told me not to fear the bees—"Go away,
bees, go away"—arm through air a rudder—

gone. But in that room reverberated
hanging echoes, melted motion, morphing

particulates of you dislodged from lungs
and then your eyebrows *were* the darkening arches

of the room—in such a staring state
I pulled the girlfriend lying next to me

from sleep, from sleeping bag, the cold wood floor.
You'd touched her hair and called her beautiful.

I asked her that she spin of melodies
a gauze for my forgetful pitted brain.

She waved her arm through silver streetlit air
as dust swirled through the window's solid beam

and on my shoulder whispered not a thing—
her eyes looked where I looked. You did not leave.

Witness

I saw my backyard strewn
with soft gray fur
this morning

that stuck in tufts
on the crunchy snow top
and wisped,

and it was strewn
with the clawprints
of many crows' feet

spiraling inward
around this: ripped flaps
of exposed inner skin,

bones dislocated
or snapped, no flesh
or very little, headache purples

and sweet reds in the thin
frozen membrane that held
to the slender curve

of a spinal column that ended
in midair over the snow
decapitated, no ears,

the single foot kicked back
and unmutilated, revealing
the identity of the rabbit.

I leave for two days
and this is what happens.
Crows eye us from their branches.

I had enjoyed her company
since the tired autumn
when she'd chew grass and weeds

by the garage in the mornings
when the crows made their noise
and in the evening owl hours.

She was not my grandmother,
had no tubes to breathe or chemo
to prop her. She died in this white open.

I appreciated her living here,
despite my never knowing
her preferences, where she came from

and whether she feared me, and, till now,
the unimaginable softness,
this feeling of absence

of my fingers through her fur.

Ice Sheet Archive

I was sitting silent underground,
shifting tattered tissue-leaves
of letters farmers wrote all
of a hundred years ago, when off

from that peninsula's ancient hoar
broke a frigid Delaware
and more—the largest iceberg
we have known, the child of Larsen C.

The dust of a farmer's gullied land
calves no more softly than that crack
of artificial color tracked for months
across a grid by satellite, no more

softly: lettered peninsular shapes
at the edges of these pages part
with one gloved finger's brush.
"Let me remind you," this farmer

now begins, in swooping trails of ink,
sharp pen scratch marking out
his losses but his assets too,
these trails a silent prophecy

that I will hear his voice, "the soil
will cry beyond our hearing or our reach
when it has gone"—the sheet limps back
over a hand the author could not intend—

the sound comes in with cold metallic smells,
oil blacks paths across the waters,
hat in hand, as wind lifts land, this terrible roar
of ink and ice, of sunlight bearing down.

On the President's Announcement of Our Hashtag

The President announced we need to keep
some carbon in the ground; he sounded sure,

his raised and lowered index finger maybe
mimicking an oil rig I've seen

on my computer screen. I caught his talk
distilled at first, a single image meme,

hashtagged to my cell phone's glowing face,
the floating phantom of a president

in light above this tiny glowing slab.
Such phones are made of matter. I forget

sometimes the way the world is swept for me,
the oil that forms the plastic, metals heaved

from mines and heavy metals concentrated
to this short-term task. I hold it here—

the screen dims—it reminds me of the black
obsidian we'd often find in flakes

along the old ravine. We pretended
that was magic, too, but we really knew

it made the body of the place we played,
the mud's black fingernails, skeletal

outcropped source of grounded mystic wonder.
That stone had been there for millennia.

Then we'd each lift a rock and toss it up
into the clicking branches, watch it fall

gleaming along a trail the trees had altered,
and catch it in our shirt-sleeve-guarded hands.

Later, we'd return the stones to the mud.
The soul of Earth is black like that, I think,

obsidian and coal and oil, the bridges
from molten core to surface, dinosaurs

to us. We listen to our President
on magic flakes we've swept from earth's ravines.

The flakes can prophesy to how we've made
an end to all we'll ever dream to make—

a human listening to the soil's voice
might speak of moderation, or of love.

#KeepItInTheGround

Out of State

Somewhere in Michigan
the creek has frozen
and the streetlamp-yellowed snow
is creased by tree shadow
where I stood
beside the broken lawn chair
left by neighbors, where I traced
another local's backbone, undid pigtails,
and thought about the sonatina
I'd been practicing in lessons.

I thirst remembering
that creek bed,
drink it like water—
a simple matter of muscle
memory, flow of melody
from tendons subconsciously tugged.

But we are graduates, and we kiss
in rooms with creaky floors.
A foreign city's wind sounds
like almost any other; your heart
keeps standard time—
I feel it in your neck.
The light from the window
falls on the piano,
which is missing some internal hammers,
and the sonatina returns
as my fingers tap
the tune of passing cars
on the small of your back.

Snow-Bound

I only desire, after brushing
teeth, after Whittier and a nap
that hit me unintended
after an early breakfast out with friends,

to sip warm coffee and eat
a cookie from the bakery,
to watch my car's curved roof
fade under fresh snow.

And all that in the fifteen
minutes between obligations.
I wonder how long these snowflakes
live before hitting bottom,

and whether we should count them
blessed or cursed. They do not
"bind" me, really, not like Whittier's
mythic family, engraved in the rural

schoolboy's recitation-brain
of my grandfather. I soon
will push through the powder
of what now falls. Shadows

are etched in their crystal bulks—
we enjoy them from a distance
when we can, dark roast on our tongues,
white missives to distract the eye.

Day Sleepers

Around midafternoon, our dreams slip out to have a walk around.

They slough off the brightness of day, cloud our vision
and take our pulses. They thumb through all our notebooks.
They read our latest emails. They eat our snacks and they know better
than to wake us in our seats. They grin toothily in shadows,
pinching us, making sure.

Occasionally rogue dreams pass from one coworker
to the other, slide hands along our human shoulders,
whisper that we relax.
                          They pull pads
out of purses, condoms out of wallets. They read
our rent checks, laugh, and suck the ink
from our cracked hands.
                          Then, with their long nails,
they trace the crow's feet beside our eyes,
noting age, fatigue, the brittleness of skin,
and swapping partners, enter us again
through eyes and nose and name.

            They charge the air with shades:
they are the hazy knowledge marked
by you, the air, and me
as we lift our heads   and wake.

Sweet Potato Elegy

The box-dry grit of root and spackled dirt
like some rock's underside turned up too long

betrays no hint of affability
or orange scarcely, nearly russet, whorled

into a joint of earth, plucked up by whom
I'll never know; it made it to this box.

The recipe you sent requires six
of "middle" size. I heft or fondle one

or two, my fingers small; these bulbous garnets
shuttling around in elbowed zags

refuse to match their contours in my hands.
The stones they've grown around are smooth and gone.

I used to think a tumor like a stone
or tuber could be lifted from the land

it lodged in. This was not so. Sweet orange flesh
of future bloom, you'll spread your steaming funk

for us tomorrow if I tend you well:
brown sugar, butter, water, life

and marshmallows melted over top
encrusting taut and dry, a linen sheet

exposing what the earth would rather hide
and what exuded mirth comes sinewy

and fast, a syrup born of baking, run
of tongue, your hands not here, your recipe.

Thaw

That kind of weather:
zip up your jacket
but leave your hat at home.

Ice squeaks under boots now
as water squirms below it, over
broken slabs of sidewalk.

Last night filled my eyes
with blankets, deep in pillows
our muffled heartbeats drummed.

Kids at the bus stop, orange light
glancing harshly over lunchboxes,
the crossing guard's beard exposed

a half block from my porch: I nod,
he nods back the distance, presses
the crosswalk button to let the college line turn

and take me off to work. Last night
we lay between a body and a cold place,
but today I see only air

and through it, colored things
like signs and trees, and everyone
awake and surprised in the eight o'clock now—

we step single file onto frozen heaps
like Shackletons going anywhere else,
our shirttails tucked and ready.

Disclaimer

We're foot-weary and shot
as we load ourselves
into the car (seat spring

creak, smell of fake fabric,
old snow chunks on the floor)
and turn the ignition, knowing

that we'll 1: scramble
to make dinner (clink of parents'
porcelain, fridge to pot heat,

kale to noodly leftover mush)
2: banter with my housemate
(not do all the dishes) and 3: sit

for hours in computer glow,
in the room that cramps
our fingers (reddening light

of windows, basement cricket
legging away, eventual fizz
of beer caps loosened, all

those blue-white Word docs), sleep
the cartilage of our joints
—but on arriving, tulips

have popped in the side yard,
feeble bulb roots holding soil,
and we kiss with our eyes open.

Another Coast

New York City

Earth Room

A Soho loft, if filled with earth,
creates an air that pushes back,
a humid sense, a smell that comes

as well to fields after rain. You might drop
onto your knees, then palms, arch your back
as if to root around, to get this smell

back home. But here, heaped on the floorboards
twenty-two inches into air, some hundred forty
tons of mass—it's heavy, it's how you breathe here.

Outside, the changing leaves broke
my heart in golden ways. November-crisp,
I nearly missed this season. Jacketed

twenty-somethings clustered on stone
benches by a fountain, caught in a block
of sunlight. Yellow translucent dance of leaves

enflamed the Village air above their heads,
below the high-rise—leaves they'll tread
next week, sunlight that fed them—they

forked store-bought salads. In like layers, leaf mold
gathers each autumn on sidewalks and yearns,
I suppose, to become earth. It will, somehow.

I'd like to lie with you in a field of winter wheat.
To smell like that, to gaze up the miles of sky
that press us back. The man who filled this room

with earth had come from California. Now care
takers enter weekly with rakes and cull
imagined seedlings, but only after fire sprinklers

feed the tonnage of what we cannot see.
A hyper-aerobic, imported ecosystem,
microbial, desires like me (and you?) the right to mold

and grow in fuller earth than this, beyond the plexi barrier,
caught in a love of light in the leaves, but held
in rooms where energy enters at angles,

reflected from the alley brick, fingering into
soil perhaps, but raked away—this earth puts out
heavy smells—squash of clod, artificial rain.

Dianthus Clavelina, Sprout!

Darkling seed, paper-thin,
consider all the growth you've seen:
a shriveled tab three aphids wide
erupted into towering green

with cotyledons bowing still
to home, a quarter inch below.
How you came to rupture, slough,
and hunch beneath my city window,

how green emerged, where pink is stored,
I lack, but there you go—imbibe
of kitchen tap, of screened sun;
a pink your darkness circumscribe.

The Gallery and the Magnet

This room of masks and blocks and of few benches
seethes with bodies here to view the sewn-up

souls of long-dead bodies caked to canvas,
to orbit through the aimless rectangles,

and all to cluster in the room next door
where churns the scene familiar. A child,

I knew an artsy magnet on the fridge where I
would swim and breathe around a town a little

different from my own, peculiarly
bright below the droopy-hanging curves

of night: the sweetly lifting billows hugged
beneath my armpits, ticklish seaweed trees

grazing calves where I would waft about
and keep my distance from the lit-up windows

and the stars that shone too big and milky.
Now bodies swarm into the gallery

to stand before that starry night. I just was there,
and now I'm watching them. We've come to see

a bit of domesticity and dream,
a place to spend some time, but while we swirl

the dust of other homebodies around
in rooms of light and shade, we're bound to float

where we have flown before. I made my humble
shuffle up to catch the curves of light reflecting sharp

from strokes I'd never seen, from scratches, egg
the color of the canvas edges, when

the man came forth—"step back"—and so I did,
but leaning in could hear refrigerator hums

of childhood: my fingers tug and snap away
a magnet from a metal bumpy wall

and to my nose I press a world that feels
or smells like someplace I will never leave,

that I will never reach, from something scraped
in ways we might not really want to know.

Breaking In

Something about the smell of leather, unwrapped
from wet protective shopping bags, strangely warm

like this room of books and drippy coats, where
raindrops break back slowly into air, an air stained

by design of glass panes, an air half full
of thousands of volumes of text on shelves less

dry than they probably should be—something of this soft
brown leather that feels almost moist because it is skin,

the skin of this journal you gave to me, you said,
for my poetry, smells almost too much

of the outside, thereby related to my bitter coffee breath
(no drinks come in the library), to the puddles of Greenwich

Avenue through which I dragged these shoes,
leather too: all cracking open and strangely warm.

Found in the City

to Monique

With the feel of your lip balm I walk through the light,
sharp distance of skyline, sun setting behind—

did we notice the foam from the Con Edison plant,
the waves licking salty East River riprap,
exertions of earthworms in cold sidewalk cracks
or chill hook lifted from the homeless man's catch?

We walked through the sunlight, gloved hand in gloved hand,
our uneven gaits catching patterns sometimes,
our voices unraveling unbalanced lines
that blended or clashed as they waved through the air

impressioning softly the far skyline walls:
the water, the worms, the city become
a room resonant with confusion and us.
We love this world so; we pour into it.

The concrete below me sounds heavy with pounding—
the light of your light in the air lifts it all.

To My Father, on the Table, Several States Away

I want you to know
your strength. It's cold
on an operating table, I
know. You know

better. It's cold here
in New York, funneled
vortex of blue breaking
into the east. You're in deep

already. You taught Mom
the snowblower. You've pushed
that engine for years, leaned with metal
knees, with rod, pin, and bone, to clear

an icy path. I want to know
your strength. To relearn
to walk. To muster a patched body
down to the earth, find a way

to sit beside the pliant slender
boy, hand him grown-up gloves,
and trowel along with him. To teach
to bury tulip bulbs for spring.

Industry

Brooklyn-bound bridge flight:
copper statue's slanting arm,
cranes of gray Bayonne –

Brooklyn Radiator

Another Wednesday, another chill
deep enough the oven's on and open.

It's two days till we
touch, bump our

butts maneuvering
the boxlike studio,

warmed by gas blue-flamed
to roast some orange rootstuff.

The sweetness and the stuffiness,
my slippers on your feet, blankets

draped, the room preheated by
my "Brooklyn radiator," and you,

with your visible delight
in toastiness and life—

I tug my blanket. Behind the wall
an alley's worth of snow comes down.

Notes from an Epicenter

Sixteen Oaks Grove, Queens, NY
March 2020

Sixteen oaks in two rows planted
down an island in the street:

school is closed, kids transplanted,
benches here are empty, clean and neat.

Auto shops still rollicking with laughter,
a boy walks by, dribbles his ball alone.

A bird keeps trilling, and will after;
the traffic, steady still, has slowed.

Sixteen oaks in two rows standing—
walkers pause, and then they quickly go.

The Letter You Sent

enters like ocean air
from windows half open –

you've come like that quick scent,
its memories of swimming, of sand

in the ears – crusty tidepool colors,
this pooling in the eyes –

we fold a new envelope, wipe the salt,
and hope to see you again very soon –

we follow your tang on the air –

Still

One year, a crumpled
envelope fell
from an old file folder,
bearing seeds. I planted
the tender shreds
into a window box, not
knowing. We watered them.

A single sprig shot
from that displaced patch
of earth. Over weeks,
it radiated spokes, it
gloried translucent
beneath the window screen,
until the day that striving
living inch bent over at the base.
Damped off, I'm told. Did I
overwater? Perhaps there was
a fungus I could not foresee,
perhaps a million things.

I'm sorry; that story doesn't really help.
I don't know what to say. We tried
to sow *de copia*, we reaped *sententiae*.

Nothing is born
still. All in motion,
and we are moved. Still,
so much we bear.

Here, what was a prebloom
growing greenness. Here,
a scoop of living earth
filled with seeds long planted.
How to keep casting.

Outside grows a sapling,
a ring of marigolds. Our eyes
swim, spring-stung, our tears,
pollen-hung, we cast,
and in this word's mad orbit
we hold each other, still.

Climate Signals, Sunset Park

*after Justin Brice Guariglia's
public art installation, Brooklyn*

The traffic sign flashes
pointillistic messages
into the sloping night—

two boys speak softly
in Spanish, sitting
against the weighted base—

its signals, warnings:
    CLIMATE CHANGE AT WORK,
    VOTA ECO LOGICAMENTE,

HUMAN AGENDA AHEAD
—clouds mirror a feeble
urban glow in gray,

skyline a distant centipede
of luminescent scales, concealing
mown grass, delayed autumn, soft murmurs.

Thunder and Lilies

Four-thirty Thursday morning and the atmosphere
rips, shudders, and blows over the city,
patters the window, booms close enough to make
something in the ceiling buzz. I think again

of ancestors who immigrated from Ostergotland's
woods and speckled lakes, seeking better rootage,
to "New Sweden," State of Iowa, land of sky
and grass and tarpaper shacks, nothing they knew

to build a home with. Imagine the heavy
wetness and crash of a thunderstorm
in a sod house. They took a new name,
a cipher evoking a stream that flows

through blue flax blossoms. Linseed cultivation
was not for this New World. Grandpa Linstrom
recalled the subsequent Nebraska farm, the nightly chore
of irrigation: he'd lift the wooden check to loose

the water from the co-op's ditch,
then walk to the bottom of the cornfield
to lie below the swaying stalks and stars and wait
for the trickling water to reach his ears

and wake him. Tonight, the sky
in New York roars, Grandpa is dying
in suburban Illinois, and smart people tell me
we might not survive the atmospheric effects

of our machines, of a kind of hunger.
Could that dreaming boy beneath the stars,
on a farm that ran without electric lights,
have contemplated such a thing? His father

would die soon after from a heart attack,
he would be the one to leave for college,
then seminary, and when he married in Illinois,
no family from Nebraska came. I knew him

as a gardener, a lover of hostas and lilies
who planted much and hopefully,
who in thunderstorms would think of the rain
and remind us that the plants would be glad.

The Day the Machines Came

We said, finally, here is some help
and for cheap. Somewhere someone
had dug the graves of a bygone age

and turned up the muck to racket
the tractor to life. We thirsted,
had no money, that day. Oils forced

from subterranean slumber became gold.
We could bring bananas back from town,
send the children to school, buy more

land, send our youngest son away
to college. Why didn't he return?
Sunlight glinted off metal shoulders,

beat less long on our backs. The earth
smelled warm, that day, felt still
soft and inexhaustible, while the prophet asked

Why do you spend your money
for that which is not bread, your labor
for that which does not satisfy?

Soul thirsts, flesh faints, the soil
grinds below the turning blade, we eat
of new cheap calories, energy dug

from deep and irreplaceable. Were we
worse sinners for what we began,
that day? Later we thirsted, needed money,

left the land to others and fewer.
We sat down to eat and drink
and then rose up to play. Now someone

somewhere exfoliates the earth
to charge our little bricks, the metals
and the heavy metals someone somewhere

has ordered from the rock,
that hands have bled against,
so we may sit to eat and play

and bend above the little worlds
that we've retreated to. When the screen
goes black, what does it reflect?

Here is help, and cheap. Does this test
provide a way out? We thirst, need money,
dig new graves and leave the land to play.

Autumn Stridulation

Temperatures break, teeter-
totter over the carbon
axis. Outside, the black-eyed
Susans stand blasted. Leaves
brittle away. Coneflowers gape,
droop anxious, stiffen. Today's chill
hushed us where we walked. We
spoke of tender things. Your hand
felt slightly icy again. The yard
heaves a late orthopteran harvest,
each pair of wings to peg and scrape
for the ear of some mate's
tibia, for us. Weird tune, I feel
you shift and tug your sheets, you
little furnace, as a tight gourd
ripens just below your diaphragm.
She feeds on you, your body
pushes her new song to its reaping.

Blueshift

In memoriam, Kathleen Brumbaugh

I.

The color blue cannot be found, they say,
in most organic pigments. Birds encrust

with sponge-like keratin their feathers, a trick
to scatter light and cancel all but blue.

Blue morphos' wings are similarly false:
their crushed-up scales will make a dusty brown.

When you first lifted up the frames that hid
my eyes, you said you never knew they were

so blue, and yet this wasn't ever true:
my iris pigment epithelium

is likely brown as yours, but lies behind
a stroma drained of nearly every kind

of pigment under heaven, clear as water,
filled with little shards that scatter back

some tricky light, another peacock fib
derived from emptiness and waves.

II.

Ben was the one to go down, slipped
like a proboscis under the blue skin of the
big lake, and all unseen his wheaty head
was lost among so many shards of light
dancing over Michigan: wave-crash then but
no Ben behind—swirling universe of sand
and pebbles churning, head somewhere some
other part should be, eyes blink see these stars,
swish of arm, two-leg kick, fast paddle to angled
sand become treadmill, he milling under, mouth
opens then because it must, ears full of grumbly
full-pool noises—lost among a mother's
scream and the lifeguard's whistle and legs
until the sputtersputter cough gaaaaasp—
hack up without help but the lifeguard walked
him back anyway, and suntanned Momma
holding him, him crying, him not to swim
in Lake Michigan again for two years,
never to touch water when yellow flew—and we,
we forgot slowly how to play in that horizonworld,
to splash back that tension line, the two taut blues.

III.

The lake I take you to won't be the lake
I knew before the baselines shifted, before
the waters filled with shards. Mrs. Brumbaugh

leaned one day behind the sinks and gas taps,
asking sixth-grade students, Do you like
that blue horizon that you've seen from blufftop

waiting for the fireworks each Fourth? Do you
remember, boys and girls, when viridescent
stripes ran out along the pier and wrapped

around your legs when wading too far out,
the gentle curling of that life, when fish
washed up in summers gape-eyed by

the scores and all the world smelled like lakeside?
The sand would carry fewer gashers then,
but some year soon those shells will vanish too,

their zebra stripes won't decorate the castles
every child today erects, studded
with tokens of insatiability,

mussels made to swallow what they've found
in tangles thick throughout our sweetwater sea.

Do you enjoy that photogenic blue?
The waves that whisper every break their death?

IV.

The extra scatter of added miles
of airy matter will daily thicken
the sunset sky to red, a wide

slice of blaze between the dark
bands of lake effect still hours out
and the sympathetic burn

of waves below. Look up: blueness
faded, the inferno of the west
appears to beat a swift retreat

and slowly, straight above, the atmosphere
goes clear. Your hands will tuck
to sweatshirt, your eyes will rise

to stars. Somewhere there, bodies
immeasurable merge immeasurably
smooth, in catastrophic consequence

contract, fuse, blow out, and spin,
and from the pinpoint pricks
of the new star's poles, where magnetic

fields are weakest, shoot the beams
that meet the telescopic earthling eye
with the pulsar's every swift rotation.

But like the lighthouse at the end
of the corrugated pier, a pulsar's
flashes, rushing brightness ever toward us,

like every star of the galaxy we see,
come red, only red, arriving only
as the bodies fade away, as space itself

(which we now see in brilliant blackness)
expands as if in infinite inhale shocked,
and all things flee from gravity. Still

supernovae merge as galactic neighborhoods
grow distant. Waves lap and fizz at sand,
ground earth, as if they always had.

V.

Simon Pokagon, Bodéwadmi, wrote
two turns of century ago, on leaves of bark,
about the bluff we stand on now. Its name
was Ishpeming, the place where Kija Manito,
that Great Spirit, chose to set his throne,
from where we know he ambled north
at night, the stars alight in Tchibekana,
the Galaxy on High, scattering the land
with seven billion stones of every color,
shape, and size. "No such charming stones,
excepting those, could anywhere be found
around all the shores of the Great Lake."
He later planted flowers in the forests,
one by one, and then returned to work
the great conceptions of his soul, kitchichang,
along the dune of Ishpeming. He built
a bow at least two arrow flights in length,
his mitigwa, and laid it gently out
along the bluff, where he began to paint it.
Far behind him, from the setting sun
a cyclone dropped and swept across the lake,
wawsaw mowin flashed across wawkwi,
anamika boomed with tigowog,
the rolling waves, reaching then the shore
and glorious painted bow. The earth shook,
dunes slumped against the bow (the bluff
we know), and Kija Manito smiled in the teeth
of the storm. When it retreated to the darkened

east, between its lingering shade and what
remained of evening's crepuscular light, he blew
a tearing squall to lift the painted bow
and it ascended to the place between
the clouds and twilight, arrowless and empty,
no string or quiver, tips in treetop glow,
a bow of peace, he said, as a reminder.

VI.

The lake I take you to won't be the lake
that swallowed Ben among a verdant throng,

that Pokagon would dream of seeing lifetimes
hence—Lake Michigan the source of life

and culture, waving on. This lake is blue
and clear as all unpeopled sky with light,

blue of emptiness, a stroma blue
bereft of pigments that it knew so long—

the Potawatomi received the tale
from the Odawa, wrote Pokagon,

who had learned it from the Mashkode
whom they had driven from the land one half-

millennium ago. Nikonong, the place
was named: beautiful sunset. Much farther still

into the drifting past the lake had worn
its flowing dress of algae and its fish—

Whitefish, Herring, Muskellunge—and never
known a zebra mussel's sharp-shelled

gash. The shells themselves are growing sparse
of late, the castles every child today

erects in shade of Ishpeming are barer
than they've been. I don't know what I want

for you to see; the lake I take you to
might wash into your memory, or rush

in roars of shipwrecking blue; I want for you
to feel the riptide in your calves, the cool

below the fire, to spy the minnows' trace
of lacework in the shallows, scoop of beetle

back-floating away for you to save to shore
and more of power and of passing grace,

but not to love the blue, my dear, the blue
that hits our pupils rushing fast, that scorns

the fleeing redshift stars, that comes at noon,
the blue that chases faster than retreat

accusing us of our own empty sails,
self-crashing blue that churns the rocks to silt

and brightens every tourist's photograph,
dark blue that lifts a tourist from the pier

and drowns him every year, that rocks or swathes
each day of death, of surf, of grief, of breath.

By Another Road

After Ida

We were confused by the roar
of the sea and the waves. You left
the crowd at Jamaica Center;

there was no room on the platform,
no trains to the city. We stayed home
from work and waited. What we did not know:

between us and the nearest subway stop,
a woman, 45, and a man, 22, that night
had drowned by the roar of the very heavens

come down. Street turned river, basement
become seabed—climate buried our neighbors.
What we somewhat knew: out West, fire

licked trees and leaped, spiring,
like fig leaves in spring. Yes, the distance
may have felt like distance. Oh, teach

the humble your way. We are weighed
down. Still we wonder what it would mean
to plant a branch, grow a tree,

gather the rainwater. Life or death.
The weather lessens, a spider huddles
under a leaf of grass. It waits for the Sun.

Waulking Song

No one's ever prepared for this,
my father told me, smiling. I cradle
in my hands your six months'

cantaloupe of a belly, until she kicks.
The day before he died, hospice-sunken,
Grandpa could barely speak: *I love you*

so much, and *Don't you worry about me*, phone to ear,
and somewhere in the house, the clock he built
chimed in its weary, regular way. And you

were in your first trimester, so he never knew.
What is best? Today we unpacked new ornaments
of wood and straw that we hope she'll help us

hang on the tree someday. So, we prepare the way,
we light candles, we sit in darkness
and in the shadow. *He was ready*, I remember

my cousin said. In Scotland, I read, women
sang "waulking songs" to pace themselves
as they fulled new wool, scouring with earth

or fuller's soap, milling to thicken
the fiber. Strip the oils, strengthen the cloth.
We're left here in a wilderness way, crooked

and on tenterhooks, so we sing a waiting song
to keep the time (and she can hear us now),
we cry out to the pregnant dawn
and whisper the mystery of her name.

Benefit

The artificial log was burning, birds
lay sheltered in the upper arms of trees,
and books were passed around to check the words
of carols half-forgotten that we'd need.

For joy we sang, as cocoa, wine, and cider
cooled, and those who had began to share
the scarcer drinks, while lifting voices higher.
Past our understanding, the knitted air

converted shame to praise. Now who could say
the reason each was really there? To raise
a dollar for the poor, to find a way
to conjure holiday relief? To escape?

As we brooded, another song would bring
out sudden tears and cause us all to sing.

A Fulfillment

Candles flicker, the tree glows,
and somewhere, the proud, scattered

in the thoughts of their hearts, think
of thrones and sacrifice. Candlelight

and treesmell, and here, the child
in your womb leaps, we say, for joy.

A pocket screen flashes another headline,
taillights slide red along the windowpane

among the scattered lights reflected
from the fragrant tree, and we,

we hold each other. We grip friends' shoulders
as they step inside and shake the chill,

and we sing, for the leaping sweet unborn,
the ancient song—cast down

the mighty, lift the low,
fill the hungry, and leave

for empty those rich whose scattered
thoughts are lost. We arrive

from far lands, but all of us, and every
one, share origins that are from of old,

from ancient days. In this flickering
room we prepare a body, and she

will someday step into this song's night,
glow within a new tree's light,

and the circle of the souls of old
will magnify her song.

What Child

The car door clatters open
with rushing tunnel sounds
and before it can close, he's begun,
the subway violin Greensleeves man.

He starts the same as every year,
arcs his way up those first four notes
sweetly enough, sweeps the trapped
passengers to his purpose: *What child is this—*

but, as always, he holds that *this*,
a menacing fermata: it sours
in ragged crescendo before the flip
as he drives back down the scale

and up again, too fast, the same minor-key
coaster he rides amid these tight-scarved,
buttoned-up commuters each December. We
all have noticed him now: hair greased back,

tattooed bulges wrap lean arms and rags
enfold his punk-rock angled limbs
as he sways, incessant, hard, wincing,
meeting no one's gaze. A light pouch dangles

by its drawstrings from his slashing bow's frog;
each downward jab defies donation
until he finishes. One year I dropped him a dollar:
his grimace and "thanks" dripped acid.

He does play well, I've thought, as he traces
that resinous darkness, descended of Tudor
plaster and candlelight, with tonal warmth reset
to his own manic pace. Again, he holds

whom angels greet—and knows
no angels ride this train. Seraphs
shield their eyes. It's unclear
why he does this, curdling a yuletide

tune each year, then marching down
the aisle, car doors clattering
and mothers exhaling in his wake,
asking us, what child is *this*,

what star have we missed, what
stable birth, what cattle's low, and who
will greet, in a midnight sky's bright stillness,
with peace, goodwill to him?

The Life Was the Light

Creation

In the beginning, before firelight
revealed the circling cave walls, causing
charcoal figures to dance, before

the dinosaur, we say, even before
the proper acids in a seaside pool
shocked together into helix marriage,

unimaginably before, light more pure
shone into fullest darkness, and out
poured all the messy matter and motion

we'd know. In that expanding moment
that created all the worlds, we imagine,
somehow, a slightest gesture, fullness circled,

a quiet word, a *peace*.

Child

Meanwhile our world roils, another cauldron time,
perhaps the first we've known. The sea roars
through a basement apartment ten blocks away

and claims our lives. We wonder what to do.
In treesmell and the silences we imagine
a child, born to earth and roughage,

who somehow, like any baby ever born,
once cleaned and fed, falls asleep,
and his fingers grip yours impossibly hard.

Across the Waters

> *"In the beginning! Yes, I know, it was*
> *holy then. The forces of eons shaped it:*
> *still was it holy. The forest came: still*
> *holy. Then came the open fields."*
> –*L. H. Bailey,* The Holy Earth

What to do. Somewhere the floods
clap their hands, and another child
is born. We stand by windows

remembering the distant and the nearer
pasts, grip them like children. If babies
know fullness, why may not we,

who work to cultivate our worlds?
Could we imagine the holiness of open
fields, the joy song of hills, then

maybe. Could we receive from Earth's ends
the messenger who comes over mountains
(and surely name her swift feet beautiful),

perhaps our child vision would sustain
all things, flickering forth the one carried word,
and without knowing it, we would understand

that the light was life and ours to hold,
that the light shines in the darkness
and the darkness did not overcome it.

Strange Praise

And here comes the Moon, praising again
in its heavy swing, piercing silver, echoing
the Sun's song, somewhere below. The other
stars get in on the game, sing their orbits

like thumbs to wet wine glasses, even
what seems like darkness hums
and breaks out there: praise. How fixed
their bounds, how strange! And on this rock,

its deepest brines, gargantua, leviathan,
they sing (say praise!) to the beat of barnacles
and slimes that slip from in and out their tiny holes,
while far above come down the tempest skies

of fire, ice, and water, plasma solid liquid dance
in ways we name mysterious, and let us note
the rumpled land, trees gnarled wild
and trees that human hands have pruned,

and cattle leap and dance, like rats! as Dillard wrote,
and rats dance too, panthers and pigeons,
limbless snakes and birds of strangest arm,
what weird delights! (What praise!) Praise what?

You'll never speak these sounds, so let them ring.
Your ears are shut—so smile at everything.

Humble up! Cut out that conquest prurient.
Take seat beside the twelve-year-old whose eyes
see farther stars than yours. Don't try to get it.
Child yourself, put on your linen ephod. Peace,

quiet rule your heart. And be thankful! The moon
is out and loving you again. Clothe yourself
in those rays (be still!), observe your meekness
from above (what praise!), and loving, put on love.

Ungathered Words

In this hurling swirl—snow
like wool, frost like ash, hail
like breadcrumbs battering plans—
who can stand?
                  After dark, we begin
to read to tiny unseen ears, imagine
them curl in like snail shells to savor
with each torn word the remnant,
not knowing.
                  Tender shoot, you'll forget
the fullness of time as soon as you
can see. Word and flesh, grace and truth,
this great and broken company will whelm
you as you gather up, trickling in your ears
like another minor flood, like a watered garden.

Day of Epiphany, 2021

Queens, New York

The laundry machines whirred and clanked.
A child approached his mother and wrapped
his arms around her thigh. She put

her fingers through his hair, eyes fixed
on the TV, where newsmen spoke
in Spanish over images of the mob

grotesquely pouring up those granite steps
in waves and waving flags that bore
the name of some false king. The fingers

of her other hand touched her upper lip.
In my headphones, a sober senior correspondent
spoke in English of 1812, the Crown's invasion,

when that dome was burnt to ash.
But this king was not a king. It seemed the rot
was in our very land: darkness covered

it, and thick darkness the people. I wondered
if the little family at the laundry might return
home to a kings' cake, its plastic baby hidden

from the TV, the mobbing of innocence. Perhaps
they would light an extra candle. *Arise,
shine.* In the humble business of our days,

in this epiphanic conflagration, what is the plan?
Millions find the plastic child, and for the day
become a king. May he judge the people

with righteousness, and the poor with justice?
Each day another little king is frightened, a president
seeks to unravel the slightest commission of grace,

to threaten our honest routines. A scattering
of neighbors mutter, shake heads, lean against
particleboard tables, linens piled fragrant. Lift your eyes

and look around—something has revealed itself
in a humble laundromat, and we must leave
for our own country by another road.

Acknowledgements

My gratitude goes out to the editors of the following journals and magazines, in which versions of the following poems appeared:

About Place for "Earth Room;" *Adelaide Magazine* for "The Day the Machines Came;" *Alluvian* for "Leaving the Party;" *Atlanta Review* for "Pumpkin on the Porch;" *Bridge Eight* for "Church of the Epiphany;" *Broad River Review* for "Ice Sheet Archive;" *The Christian Century* for "What Child;" *The Citron Review* for "Dianthus Clavelina, Sprout!";￼ *Cold Mountain Review* for "Blueshift;" *Commonweal Magazine* for "Brooklyn Radiator," "Climate Signals, Sunset Park," "Day Sleepers," "Dear Shadow," "Found in the City," "Industry," "Motherly Influence," "Sweet Potato Elegy," and "Thaw;" *Dunes Review* for "Losing Track of the Conversation;" *Free State Review* for "Storm's Breath;" *Narrative Northeast* for "Retting," "Starburn," and "Witness;" *The New Criterion* for "Snow-Bound;" *North American Review* for "To My Father, on the Table, Several States Away;" *Northwest Review* for "Autumn Stridulation;" *Notre Dame Review* for "Thunder and Lilies;" *Roanoke Review* for "Liturgy of Next Door;" *This Week in Poetry* for "On the President's Announcement of Our Hashtag;" *Vallum* for "Disclaimer;" *Valparaiso Poetry Review* for "A Fulfillment," "Out of State," and "What Was Precious;" and *Writers Resist* for "Notes from an Epicenter" and for republishing "On the President's Announcement of Our Hashtag."

The poems in the section "By Another Road" were written as a liturgical poem cycle while serving as Poet in Residence at Trinity Lower East Side Lutheran Parish from Advent 2021 to the Day of Epiphany, 2022, and were read as part of the liturgy. Many other poems in this collection have benefitted from the workshops of Debra Marquart and Stephen Pett in the MFA Program in Creative Writing and Environment at Iowa State University, of Maurice Manning at the Sewanee Writers' Conference, and of my friends Justin Aoba, Heba Jahama, and Alexa Logush, the Space Poets of New York City. Mary Swander has been an invaluable guide since my years in Iowa and helped me see this book to publication. Sarah Burke, Corrie Byrne, and Melissa Sevigny have been especially helpful readers of my work in recent years, and I owe special thanks to Mel for providing critical feedback on this manuscript and helping me complete it. Thanks to Patrick Burke for walking me back from a bad idea and for being a good buddy. I am deeply grateful to Diane Goettel, Sylvia Jones, Nina Smilow, Suelynn Shiller, and all the incredible staff at Black Lawrence Press for having faith in this book and for making it all real. To Abe Louise Young, who set me on this path, and Allison Schuette, who took me so far along it: I would not be the writer I am if not for your mentorship, good faith, and support. As Bailey writes, "The power that moves the world is the power of the teacher."

It would be impossible to enumerate all the many friends, editors, readers, and listeners who have contributed to this volume by encouraging, challenging, and stretching my work. Most of all I thank my parents Robert and Rebecca, who gave me every chance and all their faith; my brothers Ben and Sam, who kept the garden of our childhood colorful; my wife Monique, for whom no flower could ever express a fraction of it all; and Chloe, the green shoot who was springing into life alongside this manuscript and whose imminent coming and immanent influence inspired the final section.

Notes

p. 5, Mouth o' River: name used by early colonizers to refer to the place that would become the port of South Haven, Michigan. See Jeanette Stieve, *Pioneer Days in South Haven, Michigan*, South Haven, MI: Historical Association of South Haven, 1983. Interestingly, it is also a description used by Simon Pokagon in Anishinaabemowin to describe the place ("a place at the o-don [mouth] of Maw-kaw-te [Black River]") in an essay in 1900, perhaps in a move meant to reclaim a term with roots much older than colonization and indicating that this early English name emerged interculturally. See Pokagon's *Algonquin Legends of South Haven* in *As Sacred to Us: Simon Pokagon's Birch Bark Stories in Their Contexts*, edited by Blaire Morseau, East Lansing: Michigan State UP, 2023, pp. 55, 58n5.

p. 8, Starburn, epigraph: from Ralph Waldo Emerson, *Nature*, in *Emerson's Prose and Poetry*, Norton critical edition, ed. Joel Porte and Saundra Morris, New York: Norton, 2001, p. 28. Line breaks mine.

pp. 32–33, Ice Sheet Archive: written after the break of history's largest iceberg from Antarctica's Larsen C Ice Shelf, July 2017

pp. 34–35, On the President's Announcement of Our Hashtag: written on the occasion of President Barack Obama's rejection of the Keystone XL Pipeline, November 2015

pp. 45–46, Earth Room: after Walter De Maria, *The New York Earth Room*, 1977, Dia Art Foundation, 141 Wooster Street, New York City, second floor

pp. 48–49, The Gallery and the Magnet: after Vincent Van Gogh, *The Starry Night*, 1889, The Museum of Modern Art, New York *p. 59, Climate Signals, Sunset Park:* after Justin Brice Guariglia, *Climate Signals*, 2018, The Climate Museum, installation in Sunset Park, Brooklyn

pp. 72–74, Blueshift, V–VI, "Simon Pokagon [...] beautiful sunset.": Simon Pokagon, of the Pokagon Band of Potawatomi, tells this story in his partially bilingual pamphlet, *Algonquin Legends of South Haven*, printed on birch bark in Hartford, Michigan by C. H. Engle in 1900. The text of the booklet is now available in a new edition for the first time in *As Sacred to Us: Simon Pokagon's Birch Bark Stories in Their Contexts*, edited by Blaire Morseau, East Lansing: Michigan State UP, 2023, pp. 55–8. I reproduce Pokagon's idiosyncratic spellings of Anishinaabemowin words throughout, following Morseau, while also adopting the modern practice of omitting syllabic hyphenation (as, for instance, the editors of the 2011 edition of Pokagon's *Ogimawkwe Mitigwaki (Queen of the Woods)* have done). Modern spellings and translations of these words from *Algonquin Legends of South Haven*, provided by Bmejwen Kyle Malott, are available in Morseau's excellent edition.

pp. 77–93, By Another Road: Most of the poems in this cycle were written while poet in residence at Trinity Lower East Side Lutheran Parish in Manhattan. With the exception of "What Child," they follow Year C of the Revised Common Lectionary for the seasons of Advent and Christmas, culminating with the Day of Epiphany. (Of the three sets of readings for Christmas Eve and Day, only the third was used.) They were read in worship, between the sermon and the hymn of the day. This cycle also owes something especially to little Chloe, by the time of the present publication already a full toddler, who has inspired much even before her time.

p. 79, After Ida: Hurricane Ida, which came through New York City in the late summer of 2021

p. 87, The Life Was the Light, epigraph to Across the Waters: from Liberty Hyde Bailey, *The Holy Earth* (1915), centennial edition, Berkeley: Counterpoint, 2015, p. 107

Statement on the Cover Art
White Pine: Crystal River—mid-stream

By Ladislav Hanka

The cover illustration was done as an etching from midstream in the Crystal River, not far from where it enters Lake Michigan outside Glen Arbor. It's a pretty little trout stream but often the center of controversies because it flows through the Sleeping Bear Dunes National Lakeshore, arising within the national park but crossing private inholdings which realtors, builders and golf course developers covet and where canoe liveries try to increase their allotted commercial use to accommodate the many summer visitors—all of whom covet contact with the living flowing stream. Standing midstream in fishing waders, inscribing a copper plate, I sought to record something evocative in support of yet another campaign to save Crystal River. The youthful White Pine is much like any other, and perhaps that says more than the grand statement of a hoary and picturesque ancient. So much of what we hope to achieve is about opening the eyes or heart and seeing the humble arrayed before us...life issuing from other life...decay leading to transmigration of molecules and vital energy...of spirit itself...the divine spark in everything which calls for recognition and understanding. How subtly and often we disguise our own deeper motives to stand out and be loved, or at least recognized!

I've been an independent studio artist since 1981, when I earned an MFA in studio art. My studies took me far beyond the USA—to Bonn, Vienna and Prague. In Prague, I apprenticed with Jindra Schmidt, an engraver of stamps and currency, and I could have been a counterfeiter but for the dreariness of spending one's days making money. Those studies set the stage for a life in pursuit of will-o-the-wisps, apparitions, enlightenment, old trees and some good fishing, taking me to the Himalayan Plateau, Patagonia, the Peruvian altiplano and many other places. Still, I suspect that my most successful artwork is made here where I live and walk and eat from the land, keep a garden and share intimacies with the weeds and snails.

Of the various disciplines I've tried on for size, from translation to illustration and museum design, my work in the sciences most allowed me to appreciate that my station in life is that of an artist. I have collected bird eggs to study their development, banded birds in migration studies and killed too many fish in ecological studies of questionable merit. It helped make me who I am today and continues to inform my artwork. I am also grateful that I need no longer quantify, collect, nor analyze the enzymes or entrails of living beings to earn my bread. Like Linnaeus and Audubon before me or any butterfly of the present moment, I can go about gaining insight through direct observation.

I have occasionally found myself contemplating an old tree when, as I drift off into reverie with a half-completed sketch slipping between my knees, I become aware of a soul inhering in that wall of wood erupting from the earth before me. Intellect subdued, the subtle energies become more discernible. The tree begins to expand and contract in nearly imperceptible, but very real, rhythmic pulses. Inspiration and expiration—universal attributes of all creation.

Consciousness, too, is a universal attribute of matter. This is something we knew as children and must later laboriously rediscover. Eternal verities become evident only gradually, as one assumes greater intellectual humility. I grasp my pencil and circle that simple reality of the living, breathing tree before me, pointing it out once from this angle and then with another crisp line pressed into the paper from another, closing in with word and line on the truth of that achingly simple insight.

I've had over 120 one-man shows, sell from about 20 galleries and have work in nearly 150 public collections—mostly in North America and Europe. I've illustrated books and magazines, published several art catalogs, created about 30 hand-made books, designed dozens of beer and wine labels, a few CD covers and book jackets, signs and architectural elements. I've done what an artist does to get by and remain in the studio. The Permanent Archive of my works, books, proofs, documentation and correspondence is housed in the Special Collections at Western Michigan University. Several well-made videos about me and how I work are on YouTube. Bullet points in one person's experience condensed into a resume nobody reads, while the milkweed blossoming nearby and thinking not of the morrow catches their attention without effort.

Photo: Kate McKenna, 2018

John Linstrom grew up in the Rust Belt tourist town of South Haven, Michigan. His poems have appeared in journals and magazines including *Northwest Review, The Christian Century, North American Review, Commonweal Magazine*, and *The New Criterion*. He is currently the Mellon Foundation Postdoctoral Fellow in Climate Humanities and Social Justice at the Climate Museum in New York City, and in the fall of 2024 he will begin work as an Assistant Professor of English at Centenary College of Louisiana. He also serves as the Series Editor of The Liberty Hyde Bailey Library for Cornell University Press, reintroducing the ecospheric writings of fellow South Havenite Liberty Hyde Bailey (1858–1954). His editions of Bailey's works include *The Nature-Study Idea and Related Writings* (Cornell UP, 2024), *The Liberty Hyde Bailey Gardener's Companion* (coedited; Cornell UP, 2019), and *The Holy Earth* (Counterpoint, 2015). John holds an MFA in Creative Writing and Environment from Iowa State University and a PhD in English and American Literature from New York University. He lives with his wife and daughter in Queens.